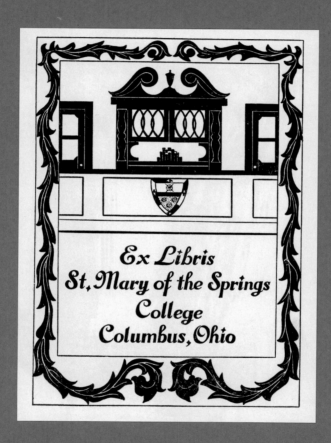

The Gull's Way

the herring gull Larus argentatus

The Gull's Way

Louis Darling

photographs and illustrations by the author

WILLIAM MORROW AND COMPANY   NEW YORK 1965

THERE IS AN ISLAND

Nine miles off the coast of Maine there is a special island. It is unique. Actually no two islands are ever quite alike; each is a world in itself, quite simple when compared to the complex mainland. This is especially true of the emergent islets that lie off the mouth of Muscongus and Penobscot Bays. Laving their shores, flowing around them, are the rich pastures of the sea on which phalaropes bob in August and where whales may be seen in their passage.

The climax of any Audubon boat trip out of Muscongus Bay is Little Green, our special island, where once, with a group from Hog Island, we saw what may have been an Eskimo curlew, one of the last of its race, bound for Patagonia. In former days laughing gulls and arctic terns bred there, but no longer; islands are seldom static. Little Green is now the home of herring gulls, blackbacks, many eiders, savannah sparrows, a few Leach's petrels, and a pair of ravens.

In this oceanic Eden, with seabirds as neighbors, Louis Darling pitched his tent and settled down for an extended period to ponder the ways of herring gulls and other inhabitants of the island. He was joined later by his artist wife Lois, and they have returned for shorter visits in succeeding years.

Unlike most other wildlife artists and interpreters, Louis Darling is a working scientist as well. He is not content merely to digest the researches of others. This gives his work an authenticity seldom attained by other popular nature writers. He intends to return to Little Green every summer until his curiosity about this microworld is satisfied—if ever it will be.

ROGER TORY PETERSON

Foreword

The behavior of no animal is completely understood. It is but vaguely comprehended for most. So if one tries to tell the story of its life from the animal's point of view, it is constantly necessary to fill in the gaps with imagination that must deliberately seem to be fact. But when a human is present to observe, report, and to try to interpret, this difficulty is avoided and reality enters. Something of the struggle to understand, something of the special relationship between the observer and the observed, something of the speculation, the sentiment and fondness for the subject,

5

and the pitfalls and the excitement of investigation can be introduced. This is what *The Gull's Way* tries to be—not a "science" book or an imaginative tale of the life cycle of the herring gull, but the story of a few weeks in the lives of the watcher and the watched told in words and pictures that have originated in experience.

In this endeavor, as well as in my continuing island study project, many people have been of inestimable help. First my thanks go to those who fish the island's shores, wander over its slopes and beaches, camp on it, and love it: Sherwood and Gwen Cook (who also own it) and their family, Hartford and Marge Cook and theirs, and Hollis and Gladys Chadwick. If one can thank things made of wood and metal, I include here the *Terry Jeanne* and the *Gwendolyn J.*, slim white lobster boats that, like many watercraft, are peculiarly alive. Dr. Roger Tory and Barbara Peterson are unfailingly helpful, and Roger's wisdom about birds and their surroundings in general and about painting and drawing them in particular has influenced and aided everything my wife and I do. Dr. William Drury has given much help and advice about past, present, and future gull watching. Roland Clement was one of the first to see my pictures and discuss some of the problems. Paul and Marion Hannemann's hospitality at Mosquito Head is an inspiration, and Marion has brought much of the lore of the birds of Maine to us. Dr. Ralph Palmer made a study of the island in 1937 and

6

his unpublished report has given historical perspective to its flora and fauna. Observations, through the years, by Carl Bucheister and the staff and students of the National Audubon Society's Hog Island Camp have been valuable in this respect as well. I would also like to express my gratitude to anonymous lecture audiences for hearing me through and involuntarily testing what was interesting and meaningful and what was not.

No one can even fleetingly consider the way of gulls without giving thanks to Dr. Niko Tinbergen for his classic *The Herring Gull's World*, as well as for his many other books and reports of researches. He has done so much in a more general way toward understanding the interworkings of the mind, body, and environment that the human debt to him is beyond evaluation. However, since neither he nor any of the above named has read this manuscript, none can in any way be held responsible for its contents.

Last, best thanks go to my patient wife, Lois, who, aside from spending many days on the island and hours in the blind, cooking scores of difficult meals on a wind-tortured primus stove, and shivering through many a night in a fog-shrouded tent, *has* read the manuscript and is decidedly responsible for much that this book contains.

7

CONTENTS

1. Island

The island is a small one, only a little more than thirty
acres at high tide. Its backbone of rock ledge tilts up out of
the sea. Rising to the northwest, the ledge breaks off abruptly
into low cliffs with a jumble of broken slabs of rock, glacial
boulders, and driftwood at their feet. At the island's highest
point a brass marker of the United States Coast and Geodetic
Survey is set into the top of a massive, weathered chunk of
granite. Although the boulder is only forty feet above sea
level, its isolation makes it a lofty peak from which the whole
world seems to come into view as one turns slowly through

11

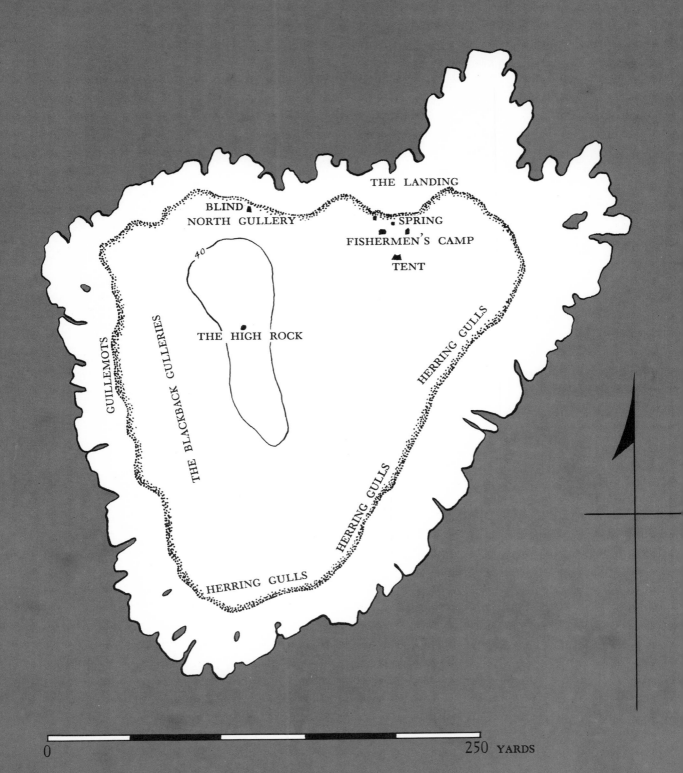

THE LANDING

BLIND
NORTH GULLERY
SPRING
FISHERMEN'S CAMP
TENT

40

THE HIGH ROCK

GUILLEMOTS

THE BLACKBACK GULLERIES

HERRING GULLS

HERRING GULLS

HERRING GULLS

0   250 YARDS

the four points of the compass. From it one can look down along the soil-covered ledges to the southeast and see the low, rocky beach where surf from the whole broad width of the Atlantic roars and boils white, day in, day out.

The island is actually one big, sloping meadow of wind-bent grass and stunted herbs. All around the shore and here and there through the grass, its dark skeleton of stone shows itself. There is no tree, no woody plant, larger than the meadowsweet or the wild rose. But it is early June now, and there are flowers—white yarrows, golden-petaled silverweeds, and the small, crisp blossoms of chickweeds and pinks. They grow all along the shoreline, where the grass is short from the effects of salt spray and the sheep grazing of other years. There the soil is thin, but rich with the fertility of the sea concentrated in the droppings of the seabirds. In boggy spots the blue flag, *Iris versicolor*, will flower soon. Even on the bare beach, among pebbles and rocks that seem too barren to support a living plant, there are splotches of dusty green where seaside mertensia sprawls. The entire island is richly green as only fog and rain and sea damp, taking turns with strong northern sunlight, can make plants green.

The island is also alive with birds. In the longer grass sturdy female eider ducks brood their olive-tinted eggs—eggs resting warmly in the breast-pulled fluff of the famous down with which the nests are lined. Little black guillemots with crimson feet posture and cry to one another out on the surf-

13

circled rocks of the western shore. At times a half dozen or so of them follow the leader in a swift underwater chase. Their white wing patches flash in the gray sea as they dive and dart and swoop in the water, more gracefully than they ever fly in air.

An elf of a new-hatched spotted sandpiper teeters and bobs on a pebble just as its guarding parent teeters on a stone nearby. Island song sparrows pour out their music from singing perches on old lobster crates, traps, snags, or any other elevated piece of wave-cast flotsam. In the interior—if so small a bit of land can be said to have an interior—savannah

sparrows nest in thick hummocks of last year's grass. A hatchling raven gapes for food from its nest of matted sheep's wool and sticks.

A couple of pairs of cormorants, barn swallows, and even a small gang of starlings in the old tumble of the fisherman's shack, build their nests or tend their eggs or young. In two of the marshy spots, nest-guarding male redwings flutter and hover. Visiting birds, wandering birds, traveling birds, and lost birds turn up constantly. Troops of semipalmated sandpipers stop off to glean the low-tide beaches as they make their way to the far arctic breeding ground. A red-breasted nuthatch works the dark ledges of metamorphic rock just as it would creep up and down a tree trunk in its usual wooded home. Jays and flycatchers rest on the island, or, perhaps, a blue-winged teal, a bobolink, a great blue heron, and many another improbable bird lost or delayed on its way somewhere else. At night storm petrels give their wild-sweet cries as they come in to dark burrows to relieve their brooding mates for their turn at days of foraging in the North Atlantic.

16

On the island's highest places, where the growth is short and the rocky ledge protrudes, dignified black-backed gulls calmly stand or brood their eggs, afraid of no bird. But the soft gray and immaculately white herring gulls dominate the island by the force of their number. All around its circumference among the jackstraw tumble of driftwood, weeds, and beach boulders, just beyond the reach of high tide's wash and spray, they nest. Bird after bird sits quietly while its mate dozes close by, or hunts along the island shores or in the nearby sea. Sometimes a screaming horde of gulls pursues a lobster boat as the fisherman, tired and done with this day's hauling, empties bait bags and cleans his cockpit. Sometimes a single bird will trumpet with head thrown to the sky. Then bird after bird joins in until the island rings with seagull music. Sometimes white clouds of birds rise and lift over the island and race downwind and wheel and turn again, just for the plain joy of being wind-borne gulls.

2. Courtship

A month before two humans had come to the island at dawn in a small lobster boat. They brought a tent, blinds, a sleeping bag, food, cameras and film, notebooks, bird bands, traps, and other equipment without end, or so it seemed as they staggered with it up the wrack-slippery, rock-strewn beach where the calm morning sea had allowed them to land the skiff. They chose a grassy spot for the tent, where there were no nests, and dropped their loads. Then the lobster fisherman hurried off to tend to the hauling of the traps while the sea was quiet. When the fog came in, at first in scattered banks and windblown wisps, the man who stayed behind looked up from making his camp for one last sight of the white boat. It lay, still for a moment while a trap was hauled, off the rocky reefs to the north. Then it was half gone in a tattered shroud of gray. It showed clear again as the mist blew by, and there was a faint white splash as the fisherman let the rebaited trap slide overboard. Then the boat disappeared for good in the dense Maine fog. Now the man was as alone as one can be, with no sight or sound of another human being possible.

For a day or two the loneliness was intense, and the man occasionally spoke aloud to himself or to the birds for com-

19

panionship. But then the feeling became a pleasant one of privacy and independence. He thought of his isolation only occasionally when he woke at night and heard the petrels cry in the wind over the tent. He had come here to watch and study the lives of the island birds and his whole mind was with them. Their affairs had become his and a part of his life.

Soon after coming to the island he had noticed the gull pair upon which he would concentrate his attention. He was especially aware of them because they seemed a little more advanced in the cycle of courtship rites than the surrounding birds. But he was also attracted to them because one of the pair, a female to judge by her delicacy of head and smaller size, wore the bright aluminum leg band of the United States Fish and Wildlife Service on her right leg and his own worn green plastic band on the left. He had placed these markers on her, along with a couple of hundred other sturdy gull chicks, just before she was ready to fly from this same beach four years before.

So he set his blind near this pair and the rough beginning of their nest. He marked the place *Nest* (A) on his developing map of the gullery and referred to these gulls as (A) birds in his notes. The banded female was the first of the young gulls— gulls he had held in his hands so many years ago—that he had seen again himself, although the Banding Office of the Fish and Wildlife Service had notified him that several had been found at various times and places. Two years ago a

21

aluminum Fish and Wildlife Service bands

plastic color bands

friend who was acquainted with his project had seen a gray immature gull with a green leg band scavenging for gurry off the Portland fish docks. That was all. So he was anxious to see what would become of this bird that had survived all the dangers that life offered for a gull—storms and cold, men with guns, oil-fouled water, and a thousand other big and little threats. He was somehow instantly fond of her, as though she were *his* bird. He was eager, too, to follow the continuing thread of her existence through her chicks.

22   Many gulls, he knew, stay mated to one another for years, although they are not known to associate with each other outside of the breeding season. Perhaps it is the fact that gulls usually come back to the same breeding ground each year,

the birds at (A) *nest*

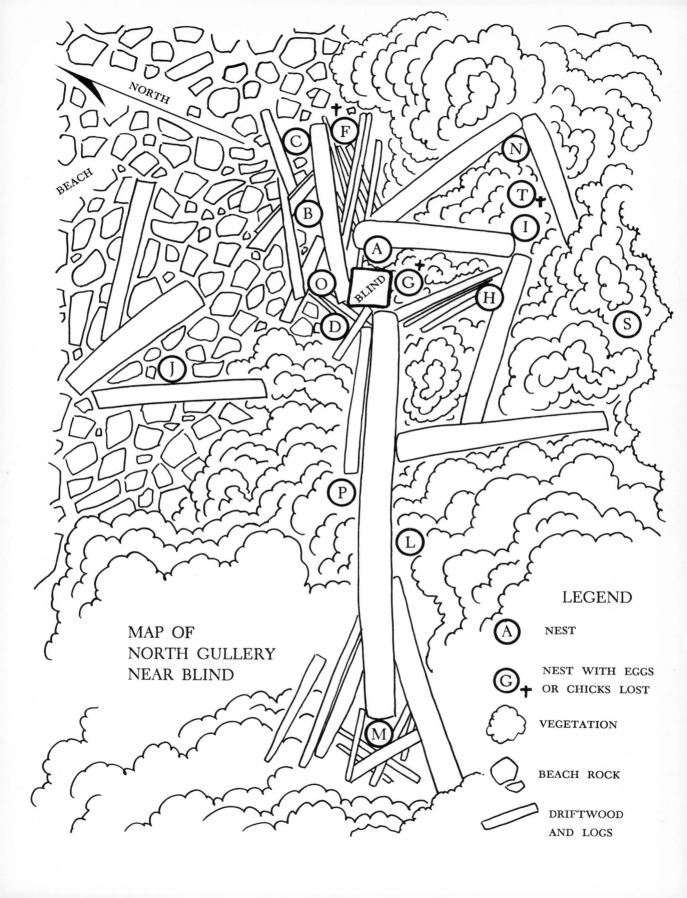

NORTH

BEACH

C

F

N

T

I

B

A

S

O

G

H

D

BLIND

J

P

L

MAP OF
NORTH GULLERY
NEAR BLIND

M

LEGEND

A NEST

G NEST WITH EGGS
   OR CHICKS LOST

   VEGETATION

   BEACH ROCK

   DRIFTWOOD
   AND LOGS

and often to the very same nesting site, that reunites the pairs. The watcher could not know the history of the unmarked male, but the female was a four-year-old and so probably breeding for the first time. When he first noticed them, the pair had already started their nest against a great drift log. So he had missed seeing the first steps of the forming of the bond between them, which could have taken place as early as February.

The building of the nest seemed a hit-or-miss affair. The birds had already made rough scrapes in several places in their area before settling on a final site. Then both gulls became very busy collecting bits of dried weed, grass, or rockweed, which they brought back and dropped at the nest site. Often, when they were together there, they performed a dancelike ceremony as with legs bent and bodies tilted forward, they turned slowly about one another while singing a strange, gobbling song. Although this same dance was a constant part of their earlier courtship and of the making of the first trial scrapes, now the constant circling and turning about packed and hollowed the nesting material. One or the other of the birds also frequently sat in the forming nest and laid straws and grasses on its rim with a special sideways movement of the head. Slowly a snug, round nest cup appeared.

The two gulls also sat together on the log above the nest much of the time. Often the female tossed her head and gave the *Keeoo, keeoo,* love song of the herring gull. As she con-

24

the nest-building dance

tinued the song its intensity gradually increased and still increased and she rubbed the male's neck and head with hers and struck up at the underside of his bill, or even nibbled at it or took it in her own. To human eyes, the big male at first seemed almost displeased and moved his head as though he would avoid his mate. But gradually he quieted and his neck began imperceptibly to swell. And then, when the female had reached a crescendo of singing and passionate head tossing, he suddenly gulped and disgorged a mass of shrimp. The female bolted the food. Then all was quiet and the pair dozed again.

This was the courtship feeding of the herring gull. It took place frequently all through the mating period, at times even after the eggs were laid. The quantity of food fed to the female in this way was small, and hardly mattered as far as outright nourishment was concerned. The feeding had a function other than to supply her extra food for the manufacture of her rich-yolked eggs. It was, rather, a ritual of love. It helped make and keep the bond between the two birds that was necessary if they were to complete all the complex steps needed to reproduce their kind. This ritual, or something like it, is a part of the courtship of many birds, and its similarity to the manner in which the young of the species beg for food and are fed is startling. It is as if there were a link, physical as well as of the emotions—some connecting thread in the vast pathways of the nervous system—between the love that is needed for the care of young and the love of adults for each other.

Sometimes, when she was especially excited, the female thrust her beak deep into her mate's throat even before the food appeared from his crop. At other times the ceremony took a different form and no food entered into it. Both birds tossed their heads and sang the *Keeoo* song. And when together they had reached a passionate intensity of sound and movement they completed their rite with actual mating. As the union took place between the lovely white birds, so would a union take place in the female's oviduct between her egg and the male's sperm, and a new life would commence.

Soon after the nest was completed, the first brown splotched tan egg appeared in it. Although there were two more eggs to come for the typical herring-gull clutch of three, the brooding started with the coming of the first. The pair took turns, one at the nest while the other hunted the sea or shore. The eggs were not once left unprotected, either from the elements or from sharp-eyed predators. It would take

27

The color of herring gull eggs often varies considerably, even within the same nest.

Brooding is erratic at first, but becomes steadier after a few days—usually when the second egg appears.

about thirty days for each egg to hatch—thirty days of hot sun, wind, thick chilling fog, and cold storm. But the small miracles of life developing within each egg would be kept at a warm, even temperature by the bodies and the insulating plumage of the parent birds.

When the birds relieved each other, the change took place with little fuss. Sometimes the returning bird gave the long, mewing recognition call; sometimes it brought a bit of new nest material. But most often its arrival was forecast only as the brooding bird looked quickly skyward. An instant later its mate appeared out of the air with a rush of wings, and the change took place silently and quickly. A gull beginning a period of brooding first stood over the eggs in the nest and fluffed out all the feathers of its belly to expose the three warm, bare-skinned brood patches that develop on both sexes at breeding time. Then, slowly, waggling and shifting and fitting its body and feathers to the shape and position of the eggs, the bird settled down.

Often the brooding bird's mate dozed on the special loafing spot at the end of the big drift log. When the easterly wind blew with gusts of cold, driven rain, the birds sat hugged tight to nest or log, with wind-ruffled, rain-resisting feathers. On other days the fog closed in and shut the birds, the watching man, and the island off from the rest of the

29

world. The gulls were perhaps the most beautiful then, with their plumage of gray and white against pearl-gray fog, silvered driftwood, dark ledges, and green plants beaded with fog moisture—the whole enveloped by the constant encircling boom of surf. Some evenings the sunset flamed as a cold-air mass moved down from Canada. The next morning the mainland hills stood out blue and sharp, and the northwest wind capped the sea waves with white foam and then as promptly blew it off again. Up against the clear sky, where the wind, deflected by the steep shore, piled columns of upward-moving air, the white birds floated motionlessly with stiff, spread wings in ecstasies of easy flight.

3. *A Place in the World*

Aside from the weather against which all living things must struggle endlessly in this harsh northern land, the chief danger for the developing eggs was from other gulls. Parent gulls know their own eggs as long as the eggs are in or near the nest, but other eggs do not mean anything at all but food to them. Just as they will pick up a dead fish or a stranded clam, gulls will take any unguarded eggs they come upon, whether they are those of a small sandpiper, a tern, a heavy eider, or a neighbor gull. While eggs are not a large part of a normal gull diet, gulls are opportunists where food is concerned. They

31

The eggs of the arctic tern are laid in the open and are easy prey for gulls, especially the great blackbacks.

birds on the nests in (G) and (H) territories

will eat almost anything even remotely edible. Unhidden, un-protected eggs do not last long in or near a gullery. For in-stance, the great black-backed gulls had been extending their range year by year and now formed a sizable colony on the island. They are such efficient egg hunters that they made it impossible for the arctic terns to breed successfully there.

But gulls are also social birds, and no society can exist with-out rules. They are not made rules, of course, but habits of behavior that have developed along with other traits during the millions of years in which evolution has produced herring gulls. They are rules, nevertheless, and chief among them is the rule of territory.

Many songbirds have their own territory of an acre or more, from which they drive out all other birds of their spe-cies except their mate. The large birds of prey control whole tracts of countryside. These territories include hunting grounds—the space needed to supply food—as well as nest-ing places. Gulls do not feed or hunt in their territory. Gull hunting ground is all the sea and all the shore. When food is plentiful they often feed communally. At times, in spite of what appears to be constant wrangling, they cooperate in finding food and even have a special "Come and get it" call, which indicates to their fellows that a rich supply has been located.

As there is no question of food in their territorial needs, a gull pair occupies a small space that is just large enough to

33

give sufficient "elbow room" and to protect the sanctity of the nest and chicks. In the open, nests may be six, ten, or twelve feet apart. But in the driftwood jumbles where logs and planks and old fish boxes provide the same degree of privacy that sheer space gives in the open, a gull territory may be only a few square feet.

A bird on its own territory seems to have extra authority when defending it and he almost always turns back the invader. The trespasser, for whatever reasons, acts filled with guilt, unease, uncertainty. With innate knowledge the birds know very well what is what, and they soon learn who is who and where is where, as the territorial activity picks up with the advance of the breeding season. If this were not so, the gulleries would be struggling masses of birds instead of the well-ordered, if noisy, assemblies for the production of new gulls that they are.

Territorial behavior protects gulls' nests, eggs, and later their chicks. It provides a place in common for a mated pair to rest and meet, and helps preserve the bond between them that makes it possible for them to rear their chicks successfully. It spaces out the colonies so that impossible overcrowding does not occur, but it allows the pairs to be still near enough to one another to benefit from the protection and stimulation that a society holds for its members. Territorial activity, seen among many different creatures as well as birds, seems also to have a deeper and more subtle function, con-

34

nected with the need of living things not only for the company and help of their fellows, but at the same time for living space, for a place of their own in the world.

The (A) birds defended their place on earth with diligence. They used the inherited rituals and ceremonies of their species as they communicated their intentions and their rights to the surrounding gulls. One of the most common rituals was weed pulling. This activity ordinarily took place near territory edges when some aggressive or experimental neighbor overstepped the boundaries. When such an incident occurred one of the (A) birds walked up to the intruder and stared at it with a stiff, upright pose, wings just lifted as if in readiness to strike a blow. Often this universal signal was enough to move the invader away, but sometimes the second bird just stared back, a mirror image of the (A) bird. Then one of the gulls

35

The birds from (G) and (H) have a weed-pulling bout on their border line.

would reach down and pull at a bit of grass or weed, worry it, and break it off if possible. The other gull then mimicked this performance, and back and forth the weed-pulling contest went. When there was no grass or weed at hand, any sort of twig or trash was used. Even immovable objects were pulled and shaken if there was nothing else nearby. A few bouts of weed pulling on a territory's edge usually sent the invading bird wandering away into its own land as though nothing had happened, exhibiting that casual couldn't-care-less air of an animal that has changed its mind.

36

If the intruder did not go, more violent action followed— an open-winged rush or, perhaps, some wing beating or feather pulling. This actual war was especially frequent early in the season when the nesting territories were being established. Then the gulleries resounded with thumps and angry cries. But once the territories were set, the violence almost ceased and peaceful rituals like weed pulling became the usual means of keeping boundaries defined.

The birds communicated by voice also. Gull alarm cries were taken up by nearby gulls until the whole colony echoed the call of danger. There was an alert call almost like a mother hen's *Cluck, cluck, cluck,* as she warns her chicks. Mates sometimes recognized each other with an almost catlike *Eeeeow* call. But for the watcher the trumpeting was the most dramatic of all. At times, seemingly for no reason, a bird slowly lowered its head and then, slowly but with increasing

the alert call

tempo, threw its head up to the sky and gave the breeding gull's wild trumpet call. This cry, too, might resound through the whole colony, as one bird after another took it up until the clamor was indescribable. Usually the birds seemed to give this call for the sheer joy of being alive, for the joy of being gulls. But often the call was clearly territorial, as if the birds were proclaiming, "I am a proud breeding gull. This is my spot on earth—a place for me and my mate alone!"

Very occasionally some aggressive pair shoved in between two established areas and tried to squeeze out a third territory where there had been but two before. This behavior upset the

entire neighborhood. The thud of wing blows resounded, and the eggs in several nests might be broken and eaten in the scrimmage. Usually those of the aggressive birds went first. But the breeding pairs all about the storm center might suffer in one way or another from such a breakdown of society. Serenity and the breeding efficiency that went with it did not return until the intruding pair were ejected, or the other gulls recognized the new territory and accepted it.

Another ritual often occurred when a mated pair defended their home together. The two birds did not aim the defense directly at the invader. Instead, when the strange bird approached their territory, they did the circular dance of courtship and nest building, bobbing their heads and giving choked, gobbling cries. It was truly a ritual of defense, however, as it was often used long after the nest had been completed and had eggs in it. To the watcher it seemed that the birds were saying, "Go away, please. Can't you see that this is our nest, our home?" The invading bird almost always retreated.

Thus the gull arguments were settled as the colony territories were established and constantly redefined. The most serious damage ever done to any bird was the loosening of a few feathers in the early stages of territory formation when boundaries were often in dispute. But the (A) birds did not experience much conflict with their neighbors. The big log to the northeast and two lesser logs to the west crossed each other and formed a protective triangle of wood. It was a well-defined territory and easy to defend.

41

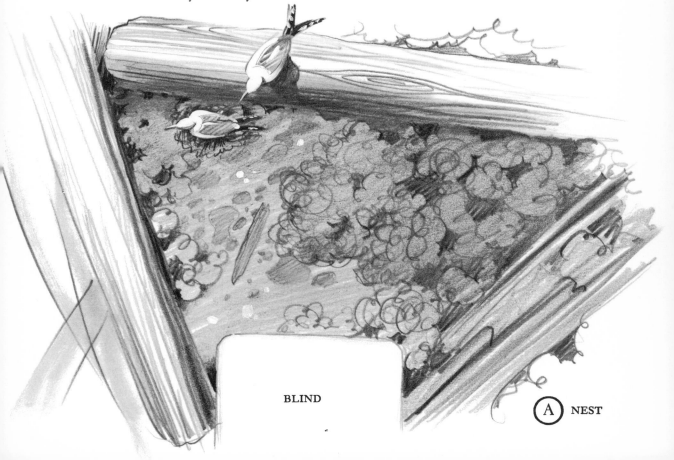

BLIND

(A) NEST

4. Hatching

The gulls continued to brood their eggs, day in and day out, protecting them from the heat of the sun as well as from the cold of night and the gray, rainy days. Sometimes, as he watched the birds on (A) nest, the man wondered that any living things, especially such quick and active creatures as birds, could have such patience. The birds were eager, almost avid, to commence brooding when they relieved one another. The brooding bird sat still hour after hour, with no hint of impatience. It shifted now and then, and occasionally raised its head and gave the trumpet call. At even rarer intervals it

42

stood, put its head down, and shifted the eggs. But for the most part the brooder simply sat and sat and sat, huddling as cold rain pelted its wind-ruffled feathers, or panting in the hot sunshine with open beak.

One afternoon as he came to the blind the watcher stopped and examined the eggs in (A) nest. One of them had the faintest star of cracks in its shell toward the large end. The next morning the same egg was even more cracked, and in one place a small triangular bit of shell had been completely broken away. The egg was pipped. The man held it to his cheek and felt the life move inside it like a warm caress. He heard a small cry. Then he returned the egg quickly to its place in the nest and entered the blind.

43

Inside the brown blotched egg the gull chick struck the shell again with the sharp cone of its egg tooth. Again and again, a thousand times more all through this day, the small unhatched seabird struck and struggled. Slowly the large end of the egg was encircled with chips and cracks. Suddenly early in the morning of the third day, with an effort unbelievable for so tired and so small and so wet a thing, the chick broke from its eggshell and lay half in and half out, bedraggled and gasping in its first free lungfuls of air. Over it the warm, soft-feathered parent gull stirred restlessly. Eight feet away, hidden behind the faded green canvas blind, the watcher looked up from his camera and notebook and knew why the seabird moved.

44

He watched closely as the parent bird rose and peered down at the nest's contents, then took up a piece of crumpled shell in its bill and shuffled stiffly off to drop it well away from the nest. Now the watcher could see the new hatched chick. The parent gull returned to the nest and stood in it, again peering down between its legs. Slowly it sank onto the two eggs and the new chick—slowly as always with fluffed breast and belly feathers, and comfortable wagglings of tail and shruggings of shoulder. But now the brooding pose was a bit different from the one the gull had held when it was incubating eggs alone. Its wings remained just slightly, protectively lifted and spread.

The watcher in the blind was immensely pleased. The hatching of the first herring-gull chick of the season seemed important out of all proportion—the end and the reward of a long process and, for him, a long wait. At the same time it was a beginning, a start to another part of the story of life and of life reborn that it was his concern as a biologist to watch and record.

5. Feeding

Soon after the first chick had hatched in (A) nest, the watching man left the blind. It was midmorning and time to stretch aching muscles and make the island rounds. There were endless things to observe and notations to make. As completely as possible, he was keeping a record of the daily state of over three hundred black-backed and herring-gull nests, and of their occupants and their eggs throughout the breeding season. He weighed and measured as many eggs as he could, and noted their color and the time of their laying and hatching. He scraped into small plastic bags the hard indigestible parts

47

of gull food that the birds disgorge in little piles. Later they would be analyzed to help determine the nature of gull diets. He checked the nests and the doings of the other island breeding birds and noted any strange stray birds. In addition to this daily routine, there was always something new for him to see, something to learn, and something to puzzle over. The small island world was alive with happenings.

By now the birds were so used to his quiet comings and goings about the island that they seemed to scream the gull alarm call and fly up from their nests only on principle. As soon as he had passed, they closed in behind him returning to their nests almost at once. Only yesterday one of the birds in the (D) territory behind the blind had refused to leave when he crawled through the low flap door of the blind. The bird had simply stood there and pulled weeds at him. The watcher was highly flattered—for a moment the bird had seen him as a fellow gull!

When he returned to the blind about the middle of the afternoon he stopped by (A) nest. The new chick was now a lovable ball of dark-spotted tan fluff instead of the scrawny, wet, bedraggled thing that had emerged from the egg six hours earlier. The chick did not move as the watcher knelt beside the nest, but it watched him silently with tilted head and black shoe-button eyes as he examined the two un-

48

hatched eggs. He could not help but give the small bird a
slight caress as he left, one fingertip stroke on the downy
head.

The adult gulls quickly settled on their nests the instant
the blind's flap closed behind him. A (D) territory gull took
its place on the blind's top, which had become the customary
loafing and guard post for this pair. The watcher could see its
webbed feet silhouetted through the thin canvas. Peace de-
scended on the colony. The hot northern sun had partly
burned through the fog, and the air was quiet and warm.
Most of the brooding birds dozed. The gull on (A) nest, the
female, stirred a bit. Then she wiggled all over, almost like a
wet dog shaking, and fluffed out her feathers until she was

ragged and mussed looking and appeared almost twice her
size. Then the feathers slowly subsided and she resumed her
sleek, streamlined form. She shifted her body, and a small
head appeared between her white breast and the gentle curve
of the folded, but slightly lifted, wing. The young gull looked
up at the yellow beak of the big bird above it. It tottered out
onto the rim of the nest and spread its ridiculous wings. With
faint, shrill peepings it darted at the vivid red-orange spot on
the lower mandible of its parent's beak. Time and again it
pecked at the spot until the big bird suddenly lowered her
head, gaped openmouthed as if to yawn, and disgorged a
mass of small pink shrimp. The young bird ignored the food
and pecked eagerly again at the red spot on the beak above it.
The adult bird selected a shrimp from the heap in front of her
and held it delicately in her beak's tip. Again and again the
chick pecked at the fascinating bright spot on its parent's bill
until, quite by accident, it hit the shrimp. Instantly and in-
stinctively it knew proper food and the shrimp disappeared.
The mother picked up and held another shrimp. Again the
chick found it and swallowed it. Another and another shrimp
followed the first two until the small gull stopped pecking at
the red spot and took the food directly from its parent's beak.
In a few tries it had learned to feed as all infant herring gulls
do. It ate a few more of the pink shrimp and then, without
preliminaries, the small bird was asleep on the nest's rim,
cuddled against its mother in the warm sunlight.

50

The gull chick had pecked at the crimson bill spot above it with an inborn drive—an urge inherited as a part of all herring-gull behavior, just as physical features such as coloring or shape of head or web of foot are inherited. It had pecked its mother's beak as naturally as a human baby sucks its mother's breast and later walks. It would as quickly have pecked at a bit of stick painted red. It had simply reacted to red as all new herring gulls react in almost their first response to life outside the egg. In doing so the chick had learned the source of its food for the next forty days or so—food that would increase its weight from two or three ounces to as much as two pounds in the next forty days.

52

Once the chick had started to feed and had rested it became more active. While the sun was warm it wandered about the nest. Clumsily it tried to preen its down with its small black bill, the egg tooth still upon it. The effort was too great and it fell over backward. Then it stumbled up and, as if the outside world were too much for it, retired under the warm body of its parent. Every half-hour or so one or the other of

A newly hatched great black-backed gull reacts to red as does a herring-gull chick.

the big birds produced food for the chick. There was always far too much for this one chick, but what it did not eat the parents swallowed again and held for future use in that most convenient gull pantry, the crop.

As the sun set behind the distant mainland to the west, the fog moved in again, softly, slowly, blotting out all but the nearest objects. The male (A) bird was guarding from the nearby log and the female had just left the nest. The chick was in the nest cup alone for the moment with the two unhatched eggs. It grew cold and lonely and commenced the plaintive chittering of a gull chick in distress. At once the big male gull came and covered it. The chitter changed to an almost whispering trill of contentment, and then all was still. The damp chill sank deep into the watcher's muscles. He stretched as much as one could stretch in the blind, shivered, and looked at his watch. "Five forty-five," he wrote in the notebook. "The fog has closed in again and the gull doings are mostly over for the day—time for supper."

The gulls rose, screaming their alarm cry, as he crawled from the blind. The new chick, so passive earlier in the day, now reacted to the warning cry and flattened itself motionless in the nest. The watcher passed by quickly, so that the birds could return at once to the nests, and walked down the beach toward the shelter of his tent.

53

6. Chicks

The next day the second egg was pipped, and the day after that the second chick hatched in (A) nest. This chick learned the source of its food in the same way as had the first—indeed as do all newly hatched herring-gull chicks, whether they first see the world in icy Greenland, the dunes of Holland, the rocky skerries of the Hebrides, or a small island off the coast of Maine.

Soon chicks were appearing in many nests. It was a delight-ful time, this time of hatching. There was an audible hum of activity; the tempo of the entire colony seemed to speed. All the big birds were more alert and there were more comings and goings. At first the new chicks did not move about a great deal, and the old gulls covered them much of the time. Sometimes it was the cold that the parent kept from the chick, and sometimes it was the equally deadly drying heat of the summer sun.

Occasionally two little spotted heads materialized from under the white plumage of the brooding (A) gull. Small begging cries slowly roused the bird and it provided food from its seemingly ever-full crop. At times the small pink shrimp appeared; at other times the seafood meal was a gray mass be-

55

yond identification. Once an entire fish, almost as big and
certainly as heavy as one of the small gulls, was offered. The
chicks ate only a part of it and the remainder returned to the
crop. The watcher noted the time and waited. Forty minutes
later the same fish came up again, and this time the chicks
finished it, leaving nothing but the delicate white backbone
to dry in the sun.

The young birds never repeated the bill-pecking performance—they only had to learn the source of their food once.
Now they gobbled directly from their parent's beak or picked
up the food that had fallen on the ground. They ate vast
quantities of this fishy food and grew prodigiously. At times
they seemed to the watcher to be little else than bulging, fuzz-
covered bags of fish, topped by all-devouring bird mouths.

The third egg in (A) nest did not hatch for two more days. When it did the newest chick was far smaller than the first two, so fast had they grown. The habits and needs of the older chicks had also changed as fast as their size. They soon were wandering away from the nest cup, exploring a little within the bounds of their home territory. They no longer needed constant brooding and on warm days often spent hours in the shade of a piece of driftwood or bushy weed, while one or both of the old birds watchfully loafed nearby. As the small birds wandered about in front of the blind the watcher noticed that the second chick had a damaged web on its left foot between the outside and middle toes. It was nothing serious, only a small tear, but it helped to identify the chicks as they grew more and more alike as the days passed.

When the watcher walked by the nest and the *Ahahaha* scream of alarm rang through the gullery, the two older chicks no longer crouched in the nest or against the ground, depending upon their stillness and their broken gray-tan color to protect them. They vanished almost instantly under a driftwood jumble or into nearby weed clumps. When the parent birds returned often only the mewing chick call could bring the young ones forth.

58

Like all babies, the gull chicks were lovable things. They enjoyed play and fiddled with bits of stick or, perhaps, an old dried crab claw as they puttered about their minute world. They often practiced flying by bounding up and down, looking for all the world like fuzzy tennis balls with tiny flapping wings. They pulled the old birds' plumage and scrambled over them. One chick sat calmly on its parent's back, surveying the world from this higher vantage point, until the big bird moved. They cuddled endlessly with each other and with their parents.

The call for chicks seems identical to the mewing call used for recognition between mated adults.

All during this time the thoughts of the man in the blind turned to other babies, not only the gull chicks in front of him, but the gray guillemot chicks he had seen in dark nests deep under ledges, the close-packed song-sparrow nestlings with their huge, ever-open mouths, and the downy eider ducklings going to sea just a few hours after hatching. He thought of human babies too, and fawn-eyed calves and romping puppies. All babies had a baby look—the large head and eyes, the rounded, cuddly, baby form—some quality beyond description that made the baby as instantly lovable to the watcher as it was, he supposed, to its proper parent.

60

The third chick in (A) nest was not keeping pace with the other two. It was hatched so late that not only was it much smaller, but its needs and its behavior were behind those of the two other young gulls. The nest cup no longer was the center of interest in the territory. The older chicks did not need its protection now. The flimsy structure had slowly come apart and almost disappeared from lack of attention. Neither did the older chicks need the constant brooding and warmth still required by the smallest one. Nor were they fed as often as they had been earlier. At feeding time, because it was so small, the third chick did not get its full share.

It was hard for the watcher to keep from feeling human indignation when this helpless baby was so neglected. But it was not a deliberate neglect; it was not even thoughtless or careless. The parents' response to their chicks was largely

When being brooded, chicks often lie flat with their heels up and toes either tucked under or stretched out behind.

stimulated by the actions of the chicks themselves as well as by the successive stages of the breeding cycle. The inherited behavior, which governed so much of the gulls' activities, was not flexible enough to adapt itself to two stages of chick raising at the same time. Their behavior responded to and fitted the needs of the older chicks almost entirely.

So the third chick could not manage. It did not grow at as fast a pace as the others and fell further behind. The chitter of its distress call was constant during the chill morning and evening hours. When heavy dew, fog, or the frequent rain soaked the island its down was wet and matted, and so provided little insulation from the cold. It was not brooded enough to keep it dry. Its small supply of vital heat drained away too rapidly.

The third chick's shrill and plaintive calling did get it a little of the extra attention it needed. The big gulls had to respond in some way to the constant cries. It was sometimes brooded alone when the other two wandered about the territory or slept by themselves. At times it was fed when the others did not eat. Its distress even seemed to awaken feelings of future parenthood in the two older chicks; once or twice they clumsily tried to brood it themselves. But this care was not enough.

The watcher's life had become so involved with the lives of the gray-white birds that a sense of impending tragedy filled him. The little gull seemed like a human child in some sad, old-fashioned story—fated to fill an early grave. He knew that it was but a matter of time for this chick. He also knew that

63

a small black-backed gull after a large meal

the wide spacing in the hatching time of gull chicks might be of great advantage to the gull species as a whole, even if it did occasionally cause the loss of chicks born late. He had seen two black-backed gull eggs hatch at an early date in a nest at the eastern edge of the island. Exposed as they were he had not been surprised to find both chicks drowned the morning after a violent night squall that had almost flattened his tent. But the third chick of this nest was still alive inside the protective shell of its egg and hatched the next day. It now was a large and healthy chick.

Nevertheless, all his emotions told the man to save the small bird—to take it to the tent, to warm it, to feed it as best he could. But he would not have interfered even if he had

had the time and equipment with which to save it. Long ago he had learned not to interrupt the normal life of wild things. Their ways were different and, for them, were right.

One morning the third (A) chick was not there. The watcher found no trace of it. It was as if it had never been at all. And yet it had lived as useful a gull life, in the gull's way, as any other. It had been there in the egg while the earlier chicks had existed through their first dangerous days; it had been a small extra margin for the success of the two breeding birds in their part of the task of carrying on the herring-gull species. But the first chicks had survived these early days and the third had come along with its role already done, to mark time for a few days only.

65

7. Opportunists

The early days of any wild thing are the most dangerous. Those of the herring gulls in this rough place were certainly so. The elements were an eternal danger and undoubtedly the greatest one; a gale at the wrong time could wipe out a large part of an entire season's young. A long spell of cold, wet weather could do the same. A shift in the movements of migratory fish, or the failure of shrimp or other small sea life to appear in season could make it hard for the parent gulls to raise the usual number of chicks. The ever-present black-backed gulls, as well as strange herring gulls, were always ready to make a meal of a wandering or unguarded chick.

There was another danger, too. The three-year-old non-breeding gulls began to appear and filter through the colonies. These birds looked like fully adult gulls and yet were not quite adult. Their plumage was not all white—there was a smudginess about the belly feathers, and the coverts of their wings, instead of being the smooth gray of adult gulls, were brownish and mottled. Their beaks were only dully yellow and still dark toward the tip. The reddish-orange spot scarcely showed. These three-year-olds began to appear more and more frequently in the area the watcher could see from the blind. They "hung around" the breeding birds like toughs on street corners. And they were not averse to a meal of gull chick or late-laid eggs.

67

JUVENILE
(FIRST WINTER)

AGE GROUPS OF
THE HERRING GULL

IMMATURE
(SECOND WINTER)

THREE-YEAR-OLD

A *three-year-old gull, between the two mature birds on the log,*

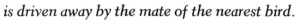

is driven away by the mate of the nearest bird.

The breeding birds knew very well that the younger birds were dangerous. A pair would not tolerate *any* strange gull in their territory, but their antagonism toward the three-year-olds was of a different sort. They were actively hostile toward them. Perhaps this was because the young birds were not old enough to have commenced observing the rituals of gull law as most of the mature birds did. Often a three-year-old landed on the loafing log behind (A) territory. Instantly all the birds in the adjoining territories would straighten in that stiff-necked threat position of the defending herring gull. The younger birds knew that they were on forbidden ground and were always uneasy and alert. Sometimes they obeyed the rules and left immediately. But often they were bold and lingered, hoping for a chance at eggs or a chick. Then the old birds no longer depended on gull formalities, but flew at the trespassers with open beak and violently flailing wings. The defense against the raiding three-year-olds was a community enterprise. Often, as a breeder drove one out of his territory, the next territory owner took up the chase, and other birds continued it down the shore as far as the watcher could see.

The invasion of the three-year-olds made the man in the blind think about the gull predation. Through the years gulls have acquired a reputation for being vicious predators. Stories about their behavior cite these traits as evil and disgusting, or more calmly, dangerous for the nearby bird life. But the longer the watcher lived with the gulls the more he learned that these ideas are not entirely true. Not only had some observers judged the wild gulls by human standards, they had also ignored an important part of the reason why these things had happened.

Gulls are opportunists, to be sure, and will pick up a meal where they can find it. They are also among the most adaptable of birds, quick to recognize anything edible and to take advantage of it. Man's unsanitary habits of waste disposal also provide gulls, in some areas, with large supplies of extra food. This has made possible an almost explosive expansion in both the range and numbers of herring gulls and great black-backed gulls. Where there is gull overpopulation the gulleries are crowded and predation is doubtless more common. However, our littered beaches and polluted waters would be much worse if it were not for these adaptable birds, which find rich food among our wastes.

But in the normal course of events the food of these uncrowded island gulls seldom consisted of the living young of their own species or even those of other bird species. For example, the island eider ducks laid their eggs and hatched their young almost side by side with the gulls. When they had rested for a few hours after hatching the young eiders were escorted by their mothers down into the sea, where several ducks pooled their young in "nursery-school" groups and guarded them cooperatively. These pods of ducks moved almost among the feeding gulls and the warning *Grrrr* growl of the female

eider was almost constant. And the gulls respected the eiders. Occasionally, when one of them got too close to a school of ducklings, the nearest duck instantly attacked and surged up over it onto its back, pecking at its head feathers, treading with its strong webbed feet, and flailing the water into a foam with buffeting wings. The gull, squawking and half-drowned, escaped as quickly as it could, and others nearby took the warning and moved cautiously a little farther from the eider flotilla.

72   Only once did the watcher see a gull with an eider duckling. One evening a lone herring gull flew high over the tent with the unmistakable silhouette of a limp duckling in its beak. Of course, it might well have been a duckling the bird found dead from some other cause. Another incident occurred when the man surprised a brood of eiders making their way from nest to sea, and frightened the mother away. The duck flew off and landed outside the line of surf, and the terrified small ones scurried for a nearby tide pool. As long as the man kept close to them they were safe. But when he moved away a little, the gulls flew in before the shy mother eider dared to return. The ducklings dived when the gulls stooped at them, but inevitably they would tire, one by one, and be scooped up and carried away. The watcher knew that all he could do was frighten the gulls as thoroughly as possible and leave at once, hoping the duck would come back before the gulls could take her brood. So he rushed at the white birds,

The female was frightened away from this nest of hatching eider ducklings.

A herring gull investigates. The head of the angry returning mother can be seen at the top of the picture, left of center.

shouting and roaring and flapping his arms and leaping over the ledges like a wild man. Then he hurried away to watch events through his binoculars from a distant hummock. The gulls returned of course. But now that he was gone so did the mother duck. She dove through the surf and streaked up over the slippery stones and wrack to take charge of her ducklings again.

The incident gave him a clue to part of the reason for the black reputation given to gulls. Almost without exception the deliberate gull predation he had seen in several seasons among the birds was caused by his own or some other human being's presence in the gulleries. He came to realize that many of the gull villainies reported had happened *only because the reporters themselves had been present.* They had disturbed the normal course of events. They had upset the protective systems or caused chicks or hidden nests to be revealed and left unguarded when the frightened parents left them. The gulls had been quick to take advantage of these opportunities.

This thought made the watcher realize that much other behavior of wild things also was modified by the very act of their being watched. He realized that many of the activities

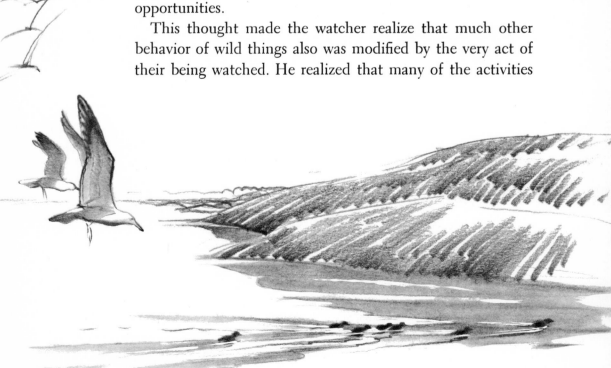

he and others had seen did not represent the normal everyday behavior of these creatures, but was their behavior when being watched by a human. So he became more careful not to disturb the birds, to efface himself as much as possible, and always to move quickly away from a disturbed area. His clothes blended with the driftwood and the rocks of the island, and he learned to make his movements blend into the background too.

8. Growing Up

The young gulls were growing out of their babyhood rapidly now. All over the island the new generation became more and more conspicuous. The young blackbacks, hatched sooner than the herring gulls, looked like broiler-sized chickens ready for market. As the two remaining (A) chicks continued to grow they also began to lose their fluffy charm. A coarser coat of feathers appeared, pushing out the down feathers as it came. Some of the down stayed fastened for a while to the tips of the new feathers and gave the chicks a scraggly, moth-eaten look. Their feet grew large and ungainly, their necks long, and their small black bills became more like beaks.

young great black-backed gulls

For many days the young gulls had also been acting, as well as looking, more adult. They preened often and their motions were exactly like those of the older birds, although the feathers to be dressed were not yet grown. When alarmed, the young gulls began to hide so well in the weeds and driftwood tangles that the watcher found it increasingly hard to check on the progress of the chicks in nests he could not see from the blind. Only by following the little trails they beat down among the weeds and grasses could he sometimes locate a pinfeathery adolescent gull. At times, however, a chick was taken by surprise. Then it froze motionless wherever it was. Whether on the sandy, pebbly beach, into which its tan-and-brown mottled coat blended, or in the short island grass

79

The coloration of the gull chicks gives such good camouflage that they are often hard to see, even when moving.

against which it stood out boldly, the small gull held its pose as though it were perfectly camouflaged. When the chicks were quite small they could be picked up and put down again without their even moving. But as they grew older their dependence upon their inherited instinct to freeze appeared to become more and more tempered with something that seemed like reason. They could stand the gaze of the man for only so long. Then they leaped screaming to their feet and fled.

Everywhere on the island burgeoning life was evident. The thirty acres fairly ran over with it. Not only did fat gull chicks swarm everywhere, the landing cove was crowded with half-grown eiders feeding in its comparative calm. Plump young song sparrows were out of the nest and now sat beside their elders on the driftwood perching places. The young savannahs were also well fledged, but were still being fed by work-worn parents. The bright yellow edging on their oversized mouth betrayed their lingering babyhood. The spotted sandpipers were stilt-legged and awkward, no longer elf birds. The lush grass was beginning to overtop and hide the tan mat of last year's stems. In every damp spot the blue flag bloomed. The more pebbly and protected beaches were spattered with the improbable bright blue flowers of the seaside mertensia. The fattening buds on the ranks of seaside goldenrod told of the quick coming of autumn. The watcher suddenly realized that this year's crop was almost ripe here in the North Atlantic. Soon growing wings would spread and catch the air

81

blue flag

and bear new birds off to wherever water and land came together in their rich, productive meeting.

The tropics are usually thought of as the embodiment of lushness and of exuberant life. But the rush of a northern spring throbs with vitality and a whole season is condensed into a month or two. Only a few weeks had passed since the last of the northbound semipalmated and least sandpipers, the peeps of the tide lines, had disappeared. But July had hardly come when peeps appeared again on the island beaches. These were the first of much earlier migrants already returning from northern breeding grounds. So fast had they completed the reproductive cycle that they almost overlapped the last of their species to move northward.

82

9. Leave-taking

Clearer weather came with July. The lobster fishermen hauled their traps almost daily off the island shores. During the morning hours there were almost always one or more white boats in sight or the throb of powerful engines in the air. When a boat came in close to the steep northern shore where the white-and-red buoys marked lobster traps lying on the sea floor, there would be a wave of hand or shouted messages if the sea was quiet. The outside world came closer then.

the lobster,   Homarus americanus

One day, as the watcher trained his binoculars on his friend's boat, he noticed that the skiff lay across the stern. Later, when the hauling was done, the fisherman moored his boat to a trap off the landing cove and came ashore in the skiff. He brought fresh supplies—bread and vegetables, and a gift of six lively lobsters in a bucket. There was mail and news of friends ashore. That evening, alone again as the sun went down, the watcher boiled sea water in a bucket over the driftwood fire. Lobster meat dipped in melted butter and the fresh bread were as good as food can be.

One last big job remained. Now that the gull chicks were coming close to the time when they would spread their wings and fly, as many as possible must be banded. The number on the aluminum ring gave each bird a lasting individuality and was recorded and filed at the Fish and Wildlife Service Banding Office in Maryland. Probably few if any of the watcher's bands would ever be seen again by human eye. Most bird bands never are. But if some of them were found perhaps a detail of the movement and travels of the island gulls or some fact of migration would be revealed.

86

Banding was an unpleasant business. It upset the gulleries more than anything else. The chicks had to be caught and held long enough to clamp on the metal band and to put on the watcher's own colored plastic ring, which would indicate to him the year of banding without the need to catch the bird again and read the number of the Fish and Wildlife Service band. Each chick had to be recorded not only for the date and place, but for the gullery and nest from which it came. Then it had to be released within its own territory so that it would not go bolting off into strange lands and disaster. All the while frantic, screaming parent gulls swept back and forth overhead or swooped at him with the wind hissing through their feathers. Once a gull struck him on the back of the head almost hard enough to stun him.

These records, when added to those already accumulated, made an imposing pile of figures. For more than two months

the watcher had been busy from dawn to dark, in the blind or making the island rounds. At times the detailed notes and figures seemed dull and meaningless and to have no connection with the magnificent birds he watched. But perhaps when all these figures were compiled and compared or added to those compiled somewhere by someone else, they might cast light upon some fact that would bring further understanding of the life of gulls and, through them, of life itself.

The banding in the north-shore gullery was left until the last. The watcher wanted to leave this special place as undisturbed as he could for as long as possible. Probably because he was so occupied with the banding and with the completion of other final records, he missed the disappearance of the second (A) chick. He had not been spending much time in the blind for the last few days. One morning, when he could spare an hour or two to watch, he found that the second of the three chicks was gone. He had become strangely fond of this particular family of gulls. He had thought about them all through the long courtship, the laying and brooding of the eggs, and the hatching and the growth of the chicks. They seemed like a family of old friends and their misfortune upset him. He was curious too. What had happened to the chick? Was the accident dramatic—like the sudden raid of a great black-backed gull? The young gull might have fallen into the tangle of driftwood behind the great log. All three chicks from (F) nest had been lost this way, but when they were quite

87

small. As far as the watcher would ever know, the chick had just vanished as the vast majority of wild things seem to do before they are ever grown—vanished without a fuss, without a trace.

Still, there was one (A) chick left—a large, bouncing, healthy young herring gull. Its flight feathers were no longer the blood-filled tubes, the pin feathers, they had been a short time ago. The vane was breaking through the translucent film within which it had formed, and the feathers were lengthening daily. The young gull preened them constantly to loosen the dried remains of their covering. And every day the (A) chick took on more and more of the gray-brown mottled plumage of the juvenile herring gull and looked less and less like the appealing infant of a few weeks past.

When the time came to band the (A) chick it was easy to catch, because it had become so tame. The watcher held it for a moment after he was finished and felt its warmth and the racing beat of its small heart against his hand. It seemed a very long time since he had lightly pressed the crack-starred egg to his cheek and felt the life stir within it.

In two months or less after hatching, the young gulls of the year fly well and hunt over the sea for themselves.

The gray-green blind, even more faded now and streaked with the white of gull droppings, had been packed that noon along with bags and boxes of equipment. All that was left was his camping gear, enough food for two more meals, the binoculars, and one camera. Next morning, if the sea were quiet enough, the fisherman would come ashore and the watcher would leave the little green island and the gulls. Now as the sun went down he looked at the bird in his hands. A hundred thoughts ran through his head—thoughts of wings over sunny headlands and clean blue seas; of garbage dumps and polluted city rivers; of lines of docks and hooting tugs and

ponderous great steamers; of wings following ships; of howl-
ing storms and of quiet, impenetrable fogs; of mated gray-
white birds and of fluffy chicks tapping at red-marked beaks
as little gull chicks have tapped for millions of years; of
guns, high hidden wires, of towers and airfields and dry
crumpled bundles of bone and feather entangled in the tide-
line trash. He thought too of the ancient sea and of the ancient rocks of the shoreline and the islands sculptured by the
ceaseless come and go of tides and the furious wash of storms.
And, as he gently put the seabird down by the last trodden
remains of the nest cup in which it had been incubated and
hatched, his thoughts went back four years to the time when
he had done the same thing in the same place with this
youngster's mother, when she had been this age. The man
turned and walked off along the shore toward his weather-
beaten tent.

It is impossible to list in the space allotted all the books, articles, and papers used for reference in preparing this book. However, there follows a short list of books recommended for further reading or for field identification. Many of these works will not only carry the especially interested student much deeper into what is known of gull behavior and ecology, they will also provide extensive bibliographies.

Recommended Reading

Bent, Arthur C. *Life Histories of North American Gulls and Terns*. New York, Dodd, Mead, 1947.

Berrill, N. J. *The Living Tide*. New York, Dodd, Mead, 1951.

Carson, Rachel L. *Edge of the Sea*. Boston, Houghton Mifflin, 1955.

Darling, F. Fraser. *Bird Flocks and the Breeding Cycle*. New York, Macmillan, 1938.

Darling, F. Fraser. *Natural History in the Highlands and Islands*. New York, British Book Centre, 1952.

Darling, Lois and Louis. *Bird*. Boston, Houghton Mifflin, 1962.

Fisher, James, and Lockley, R. M. *Sea Birds*. Boston, Houghton Mifflin, 1954.

Fisher, James, and Peterson, Roger T. *The World of Birds*. Garden City, New York, Doubleday, 1964.

Hebard, Frederick V. *Water Birds of Penobscot Bay*. Portland, Maine, Portland Society of Natural History, 1959.

Palmer, Ralph S. *Maine Birds*. Cambridge, Massachusetts, Museum of Comparative Zoology, 1949.

Peterson, Roger T. *A Field Guide to the Birds*. Boston, Houghton Mifflin, 2nd. rev. ed., 1947.

Pough, Richard H. *Aubudon Water Bird Guide*. Garden City, New York, Doubleday, 1951.

Tinbergen, Niko, and the editors of *Life*. *Animal Behavior*. New York, Time, Inc., 1965.

Tinbergen, Niko. *Curious Naturalists*. New York, Basic Books, 1959.

Tinbergen, Niko. *The Herring Gull's World*. New York, Basic Books, rev. ed., 1961.